Sterling Bits

Cookbook
Sketchbook

Bluegrass Equestrian Experience

Kathy Mayfield/Suzy Smith

13-digit International Standard Book Number 978-1-934898-07-9
Library of Congress Card Catalog Number 2010926035

Cover design and book layout by Asher Graphics
Drawings and cover illustration by Suzy Smith

Manufactured in the United States of America

All book order correspondence should be addressed to:

McClanahan Publishing House, Inc.
P.O. Box 100
Kuttawa, KY 42055

800-544-6959

www.kybooks.com

A Bit about Sterling Bits

Sterling Bits sports seasonal menus laced with timeless recipes appropriate for Bluegrass horse events, dinner parties, or casual cocktail gatherings. It lengthens its stride by including understated styles, ideas and decorating notes, all galloping together under tickling passages about famous places, history and culture of Kentucky and her people.

Complete with palate-pleasing foods, entertaining format and rich illustrations, Sterling Bits is a winning bet for making any event a success!

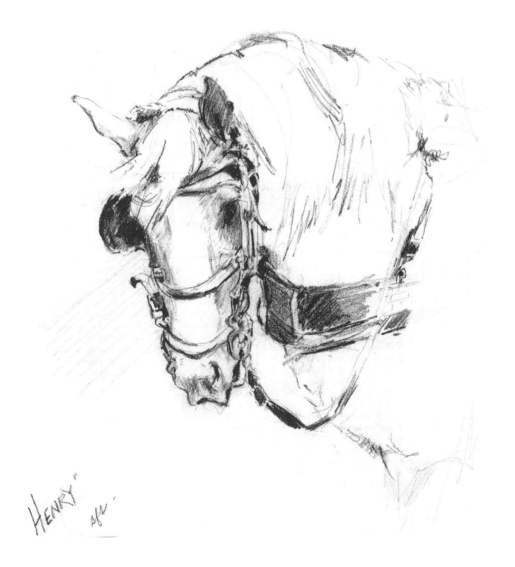

Contents

Foreword

Sterling Bits is a compilation of regional recipes, information and ideas for entertaining based on the culture and traditions of Kentucky's equine industry.

Although we've included some fun entertaining tidbits and facts, a complete work of all things related to "Bluegrass state hosses and their handlers" would be a Herculean task and more than the intent of this text. It is our wish for Sterling Bits to provide you with an enjoyable and useful reference for entertaining.

In Kentucky, it's not "Goodbye,"
it's "Come back and see us!"

Horse Life Etiquette and Safety Notes

The Bluegrass area is a horse heaven and haven. Here are some etiquette notes and reminders of what to expect when you enter the wonderful and diverse world of Kentucky's horses.

Safety is the first rule of order. Courtesy and alertness are stabled in the same barn with safety.

- Stay on the right side of any entrance, road, path, lane or doorway.
- NEVER block a gate, stall door, path, road or public area at any time.
- Walk quietly and calmly around stables, exercise areas, arenas, paddocks and fields.
- Like your voice, your hands are important. Keep them low, quiet and close.
- If you have permission to pet a horse, move toward the head from the left side before raising your hand to the muzzle or the neck.
- Horsemen generally approach their animal from the front left side and mount and dismount from the left as well.
- Should you offer a horse a carrot, oats or any treat with the owner's or rider's permission, place the food in the palm of your upturned hand keeping your fingers and thumb together and very flat like a table top. It tickles when they lift the tidbit from you.
- KEEP A SAFE DISTANCE FROM A HORSE'S REAR.
- Keep your distance while people are working their horses. If you are not in the stands or on the rail during an event or race, stand or sit next to a building, post, or other large structure, so an animal will be less likely to "spook" should they see a stranger nearby.

🐎 Avoid having any loose cups, newspaper, or clothing that a sudden breeze may flap into the air and cause a horse to shy, bolt or play "hard to handle."

🐎 Be courteous and ask a rider, trainer or owner for permission before speaking to a horse.

🐎 Professional clients, invited guests or news media may enjoy privileges and access to many areas denied to others.

🐎 Wear quality weatherproof farm or paddock footwear when you are heading to a barn, training track, workout arena, or field. Layer your clothing because Kentucky weather can change dramatically within hours.

🐎 Be punctual to your appointments and events because horses and handlers are on a purposeful time schedule.

🐎 If you pass through a gate and it was closed, CLOSE it behind you and double check that it is secure. Always leave gates, stall doors and other doors as you found them.

🐎 If an animal becomes loose or is running freely, be sure you are out of its way. Do not try to halt or handle a horse yourself.

Enjoy your visit along the avenues of Kentucky's historical, magnificent and unparalleled horse country. Welcome to the Bluegrass.

Four Kentucky Equestrian Seasons

Spring: Barn I:
> **Keeneland Race Course Spring Meet**
> **A Race Day Clubhouse Menu**
> **Churchill Downs Race Track**
> **The Kentucky Derby**
> **A Traditional Derby Breakfast**
> **The Kentucky Horse Park**
> **Rolex Three-Day Event**
> **Feedbag Lunch**
> **High Hope Steeplechase**
> **Brush Jump Picnic Basket**

Summer: Barn II:
> **The Red Mile Harness Track**
> **Lexington Junior League Blue Ribbon Box Lunch**
> **Summer Horse Sale Cocktail Party**

Fall: Barn III:
> **Foxhunting**
> **Hunt Club Scarlet Coat Breakfast**
> **Kentucky Trail Riding**
> **Autumn Trail Ride Saddlebag Grub**

Winter: Barn IV:
> **Foaling Season**
> **Foaling Barn Watch Comfort Foods**

Bluegrass air is the freshest; Bluegrass horses are the swiftest, and Bluegrass cooking is the finest.

Barn I:

Spring

sfs

Keeneland Barn.

3-8-08
SAT. -
BIGGEST
SNOWFALL
IN LEX-

HI = 27°
LOW 21°

WIND CHILL 14°

12" SNOW - LOUISVILLE

Keeneland Race Course

4201 Versailles Road Lexington, KY 40510
1-800-456-3412 www.keeneland.com

Keeneland Race Course is simply called Keeneland in this part of the country and hosts a spring (April) and fall (October) meet on it's historical track just west of Lexington. The first race took place in 1936 and the "Sport of Kings" was on its way to becoming established in Lexington, Kentucky.

The gated entrance to the historic race track boasts an iron oval crest bearing only a slightly curly K encircled by a laurel wreath. Visitors will notice the trademark color of the track, a deep bluish green paint which can trick the eye into thinking it is much darker in certain light or shadow.

This hallmark color may remind you of another famous blue – Kentucky bluegrass. In the twilight of a warm Kentucky summer, in the right sunlight and under a gentle breeze, the turn of the grass shafts against the rolling fields appear as an unmistakably beautiful blue hue. It is believed that the combination of limestone and the soil in this region results in the famous bluegrass of Kentucky. How appropriate for the Keeneland Association to adopt this as it's signature color because it has long been touted that bluegrass is just what foals need to develop strong bones and bodies.

Keeneland hosts a number of prestigious graded stakes races. Notable among the spring races is the Toyota Bluegrass Stakes, an important prep race for the Kentucky Derby which is held the first Saturday in May at Churchill Downs Race Course in Louisville, Kentucky.

In addition to an outstanding race schedule, Keeneland is also known for its horse sales and auctions.

Keeneland Race Course is welcoming to visitors, understated in class and steeped in thoroughbred history.

– 2 values
quick study

A Race Day Clubhouse Menu

Jockey's Winning Pork Tenderloin
Groom's Salad with Sweet and Sour Dressing
Thoroughbred Park Green Beans
Lead Pony Potato Casserole
Hot Rolls with Chopped Chive Butter
Paddock Pound Cake with Kentucky Bourbon Sauce

jockey's winning pork tenderloin

Select a plump tenderloin from the butcher's case.
Marinade ingredients are for one pound of tenderloin.

marinade

1/3 cup soy sauce
1/3 cup Kentucky bourbon
1/3 cup brown sugar

Place pork tenderloin in a plastic bag or casserole dish. Pour
marinade over and seal tightly. Refrigerate overnight. Heat oven
to 350 degrees and cook pork 20 minutes per pound.

squint to see
the folds in
the boot.

groom's salad
with sweet and sour dressing

15-ounce can small, sweet peas
8-ounce jar chopped pimentos
15-ounce can shoe peg corn
15-ounce can French-style green beans
1 red onion, chopped
1 bell pepper, chopped
1 cup chopped celery
1/2 cup vegetable oil
1 cup sugar
1/2 cup vinegar
1 teaspoon salt
1 teaspoon pepper

Drain peas, pimentos, corn, and green beans. Combine with onion, bell pepper, and celery in a large bowl.

In a saucepan, heat the oil, sugar, vinegar, salt and pepper until the sugar is dissolved. Pour the mixture over the vegetables. Cool in the refrigerator before serving.

Serves 8 to 10

lead pony potato casserole

10 medium potatoes, peeled
8-ounce package cream cheese, softened
8-ounce carton sour cream
1/2 cup butter or margarine, melted
1/4 cup chopped chives
1 clove garlic, minced
2 teaspoons salt

Cook potatoes in boiling water until tender, drain and mash. In a large bowl, beat the cream cheese until smooth, add potatoes and remaining ingredients; beat until almost smooth. Spoon the mixture into a buttered two-quart casserole dish. Cover and refrigerate overnight. Ten minutes before baking, remove the dish from the refrigerator. Bake, uncovered, for 30 minutes at 350 degrees.

Serves 8 to 10 outriders and jockeys

thoroughbred park green beans

Two 14.5-ounce cans green beans
1/4 cup butter
1/3 cup chopped cashews
3 tablespoons honey

Cook the beans. Drain and keep warm. In a large skillet, add butter
and cashews and sauté over low heat for about 5 minutes or until
lightly browned. Add honey and stir constantly for about 1 minute.
Pour the sauce over the beans and toss gently to coat.

Serves 6

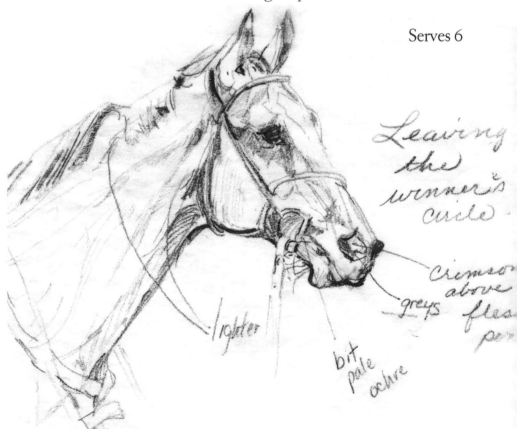

Leaving
the
winner's
circle

crimson
above
greys flea
pen

lighter

bit
pale
ochre

hot rolls with chopped chive butter

12-ounce package dinner rolls
1 pound salted butter, softened
1 to 2 tablespoons finely chopped fresh chives

Prepare dinner rolls according to package directions. In a small bowl, combine softened butter with chopped chives, blending well with a fork or a mixer. Shape the herb butter into a block and return to the refrigerator to set. Slice butter into pats and serve with warm rolls.

Serves 10 to 12

Sterling suggestion: Using commercial rolls from the market makes this bread a snap to prepare.

paddock pound cake
with kentucky bourbon sauce

1/2 pound lightly salted butter
3 cups sugar
1 cup sour cream
3 cups all-purpose flour
1/2 teaspoon baking soda
6 eggs
1 teaspoon vanilla extract
1 teaspoon almond extract

In a large bowl, cream the butter and sugar together; add the sour cream. In a separate bowl, sift the flour and baking soda together. Add to the creamed mixture, alternately with one egg at a time.

Add the vanilla and almond extracts. Pour into a greased and lightly floured tube cake pan. Bake in a preheated 350-degree oven for 1 hour and 20 minutes.

kentucky bourbon sauce

2 tablespoons butter
2 tablespoons all-purpose flour
1 1/4 cups milk
1 cup finely granulated white sugar
1 tablespoon Kentucky bourbon

Melt the butter in a 1-quart saucepan over medium heat. Add the flour and cook, whisking until well combined. Remove from the heat and stir in the milk, sugar and bourbon. Bring to a boil, whisking constantly until thickened, about 5 to 7 minutes. Carefully drizzle over the pound cake and serve immediately.

Serves 10 to 12

17 hands
if he's
an inch.

Churchill Downs Race Track

700 Central Avenue, Louisville, KY 40208
(502) 636-4400 www.churchilldowns.com

Thoroughbred horse racing has been an integral part of Louisville's historical tapestry for the past 200 years. This race course's evolving threads were woven together as they passed through many skilled horsemen's hands for over two centuries until its fabric was finally bound with its world famous name, Churchill Downs. A pair of classically designed wooden architectural structures sits atop the clubhouse's main roof line. These two track monarchs are referred to as Churchill's trademark, "Twin Spires."

The Kentucky Derby, as well as the Oaks Stakes, was raced for the first time in Louisville during the opening meet in May, 1875. The Kentucky Derby is run each spring on the first Saturday in May. It is the standard by which three-year-old colts are measured.

Only the elite of their class can be nominated for such a prestigious match. Any filly that has an outstanding record, stamina and sheer heart, can also earn a place at the starting gate. Winning the Kentucky Derby is the pinnacle of racing. Because the victor is blanketed with a mammoth swath of rich red roses, the Derby is nicknamed, "Run for the Roses."

Each year a Derby Breakfast is hosted by the governor and first lady on the grounds of the state capital in Frankfort. Kentuckians everywhere entertain with Derby parties, while awaiting the excitement of the late afternoon feature race to unfold.

On this first Saturday in May, regardless of the weather, women dress in their finest spring suits and sundresses. They don lavish Derby hats, which are typically large, wide brimmed, and tastefully styled to match their ensembles.

The day before the Run for the Roses, racing fans gather for the Kentucky Oaks Stakes Race, which challenges the finest of three-year-old thoroughbred fillies. The winner of the Oaks is draped in a flowing shawl of white Oriental lilies that are as fragrant and beautiful as the roses selected for the Derby and just as richly deserved.

In May, all thoroughbred racing eyes turn to Kentucky.

Kentucky
Derby Day Breakfast

Mint Julep Cocktail
A Winning Mimosa
Young Rider's Mimosa
Zing Red Eye
Country Ham and Cream Biscuits
Quarter Pole Quiche
Back Stretch Baked Apples
Cheese Pudding
Drop Tea Doughnuts
Bettor's Banana Bread
Chocolate Dipped Fresh Strawberries

mint julep cocktail

The mint julep is the official drink of the Kentucky Derby and is considered a true "southern tradition."

4 to 5 fresh mint leaves, washed and dried
1 teaspoon granulated sugar, or powdered sugar
Water
Ice
3 ounces Kentucky bourbon

Place the mint leaves in a chilled 10-ounce glass or traditional julep cup. Add sugar and a splash of water. Gently mash the mint leaves and the sugar together to make a paste. Fill the julep cup with ice and mix in bourbon.

Serves 1

"May your bourbon be mellow and your horses swift!"

a winning mimosa

Crushed ice
Chilled orange juice
2 tablespoons Grand Marnier
Chilled champagne
Orange segments or mint sprigs for garnish

Place a small amount of the crushed ice in a champagne flute or large wine glass. Fill half way with the orange juice; add Grand Marnier and champagne to nearly fill the glass. Garnish with an orange segment or mint sprig.

Serves 1

young rider's mimosa

Crushed ice
Chilled orange juice (freshly squeezed is best)
Ginger ale
Orange segment or mint sprig for garnish

Place a small amount of crushed ice in a serving glass. Fill with an equal mixture of orange juice and ginger ale. Garnish with an orange segment or mint sprig.

Serves 1

zing red eye

1 quart tomato juice
2 tablespoons Worcestershire sauce
1 cup ketchup
2 tablespoons hot sauce
1 cup water
1 teaspoon salt

Combine all ingredients
in a large pitcher. Stir
gently and serve
over ice.

Serves 8

INTERVIEW
IN
KEENLAND
PADDOCK
2004

country ham and cream biscuits

1 3/4 cups self-rising soft wheat flour
1 cup heavy whipping cream
Butter or margarine, melted

Place flour in a large mixing bowl. Add the cream and blend well.
Turn the dough onto lightly floured surface and knead gently
8 to 10 times. Roll the dough to 1/2-inch thickness. Cut with a 2-inch
biscuit cutter, dipping cutter into flour between cuts. Press the cutter
straight down without twisting for straight sided, evenly shaped
biscuits. Place on a non-greased baking sheet. Brush the tops with
melted butter or margarine. Bake in a preheated 500-degree oven
for 8 to 10 minutes. Serve the biscuits warm with thinly sliced
country ham.

Serves 8 to 10

Sterling suggestion: These biscuits can be prepared and frozen ahead of time. Place prepared biscuits on a baking sheet and when completely frozen, slip them into a freezer bag. Thaw biscuits before baking.

quarter pole quiche

4 eggs
2 cups milk
1/2 cup butter
3/4 cup biscuit mix
2 cups grated Cheddar or Swiss cheese
1/2 teaspoon salt
Dash of pepper

Mix the eggs, milk and butter in a blender until lightly combined.
Stir in the biscuit mix, cheese, salt and pepper. Pour into a
well-greased 10-inch pie pan or baking dish. Gently push the
cheese into the surface of the mixture. Bake at 350 degrees for about
45 minutes or until set. Let stand 10 minutes before slicing.

Serves 6 to 8

Sterling suggestion:
A square baking dish makes cutting this
quiche easier, which works well
for parties.

back stretch baked apples

4 fresh apples
2 teaspoons brown sugar
1/2 teaspoon cinnamon
Apple juice

Wash and core apples (but not all the way through the fruit); place in a baking dish. Fill centers of the apples with equal amounts of the brown sugar and cinnamon. Pour the apple juice until about 1/4 inch deep. Bake, uncovered, for about 45 minutes in a preheated 375-degree oven.

Sterling suggestion: Substitute cinnamon candy drops for an extra kick.

cheese pudding

One loaf bread, crusts removed
3/4 pound soft, creamy, velvety cheese, cubed
1 stick butter
2 cups whole milk
1/4 teaspoon red pepper
1/2 teaspoon dry mustard
3 eggs, beaten
1/2 teaspoon salt

Cut the bread into small squares. Layer the bread and cheese in a 9 by 13-inch greased baking dish. Melt the butter and mix with remaining ingredients. Pour over the bread and cheese layers. Refrigerate overnight. Bring to room temperature before baking at 345 degrees for 50 minutes.

Serves 8 to 10 riding instructors

Sterling suggestion:
This recipe must be prepared the day before and refrigerated overnight.

drop tea doughnuts

1 egg, beaten
1/2 cup milk
3 tablespoons baking powder
1/3 teaspoon salt
1/3 cup sugar
1 1/3 cups sifted all-purpose flour
1 tablespoon melted shortening
2 cups vegetable oil for cooking

In a large bowl, stir together the beaten egg and milk. Add the dry ingredients. Stir in the shortening and blend well. Drop by teaspoon into hot oil (350 degrees) and deep fry for 3 to 4 minutes.

Serves 4 to 6

chocolate dipped
fresh strawberries

8 ounces milk chocolate chips
1 tablespoon solid shortening
1 quart strawberries, rinsed and patted dry

Melt chocolate chips and shortening in a heavy saucepan. Dip strawberries into the melted chocolate and place on waxed paper to harden. Easy to make and fun to serve.

Serves 6

bettor's banana bread

1 stick butter
1 cup sugar
3 to 5 bananas, mashed
2 eggs
2 cups all-purpose flour
1 teaspoon soda
1 teaspoon salt

In a large bowl, cream butter and sugar and add mashed bananas. Add the eggs one at a time, stirring well after each addition. Sift flour, soda and salt; beat into the banana mixture. Pour into a greased and lightly-floured loaf pan. Bake for 45 minutes in a 350-degree oven, or until a toothpick inserted in the center comes out clean, and loaf is lightly browned.

Serves 10 to 12

Sterling suggestion:
The secret to Mayfield's own Bettor's Banana Bread is using frozen bananas. Place the bananas on a plate or in a bowl to thaw. Peel and mash the bananas with their own juice. Sift the dry ingredients and remeasure before adding to the banana mix. There will be some leftover dry ingredients. This also can be baked in an iron skillet.

The Kentucky Horse Park

4089 Iron Works Pike Lexington, KY 40511
800-678-8813 www.kyhorsepark.com

The Kentucky Horse Park, which is owned by the Commonwealth of Kentucky, has been open to the public since the fall of 1978. She is as beautiful as any southern belle. Consisting of approximately 1,200 acres of infamous Bluegrass farmland, she is groomed to properly stable various breeds, and to allow people of all ages to enjoy the horses, a variety of events, and competitions as well as the spectacular landscape. The preserved limestone-enriched grounds, classic wooden barns, fences and streams, as well as new indoor and outdoor arenas, allow ample room for horses and horsemen to demonstrate their talent and for spectators to witness all the facets of this magnificent jewel.

The World Equestrian Games are internationally prized because of the quality of the horses and the abilities of the riders and trainers who qualify to enter. There are eight disciplines of horsemanship exhibited: vaulting, dressage, reining, show jumping, eventing, para-equestrian, endurance and driving. Finding a location to host games of this caliber is not unlike finding a home for the Olympics. Stellar standards and logistical challenges converge and comply.

The arrival of the World Equestrian Games in the United States during the fall of 2010 is the first time the games have left European soil. Horse sense secured the event for our own world class locale, The Kentucky Horse Park. Nestled in the Bluegrass Region, the Horse Park has few peers. Lexington, Kentucky in turn, has long been appreciated by many as the "Horse Capital of the World."

Polo Anyone?

A polo tournament is a thrill. The Kentucky Horse Park is a special location for brilliant matches between highly competitive riders and their strong and spirited mounts. The schedule plays between April and October. A riotous sport, polo is the regulated colliding of galloping steeds with mallet-wielding equestrians smashing a relatively small ball on turf toward a goal.

Safety rules are strictly enforced and guidelines are extremely important to this imposing game between mounted riders and their highly trained horses. It is a time to step back and clear a field for the energetic competition. Visitors are encouraged to witness all the excitement from the grassy sidelines, while watching the skill of the players and feeling the power of the thunderously swift, agile, typically compact polo ponies and horses.

Guests are reminded to layer clothing, bring a picnic, and don't forget the water bottle. Pick a favorite team, horse or rider to cheer, and soon you'll be caught up in the fun, the intensity, the athletic player's   strategy, and breathtaking movements of the horses.

The Rolex Kentucky Three-Day Event at the Kentucky Horse Park

Held each April, the Rolex Kentucky Three Day Event is an important equestrian trial of three disciples: dressage, show jumping and cross country racing. Because the weather in Kentucky in the spring is unpredictable and the Rolex covers many acres of ground, visitors may choose to carry a picnic basket or brown bag of food and snacks for convenience.

The recipes we've chosen for this section are simple to prepare for a day at the Kentucky Horse Park, as well as other times and places when light fare and ease of transport would ride well together.

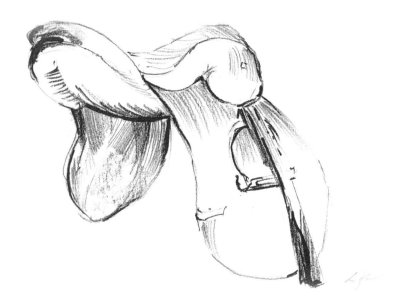

Rolex Kentucky Three-Day Event Feedbag Lunch

Dressage Fried Chicken
Cross Country Race Cheese Biscuits
Tack Box Celery and Carrot Sticks
Spectator Brownies
Lunge Line Treat

dressage fried chicken

1 frying chicken, cut into pieces
3 eggs
Hot sauce
1 cup all-purpose flour
2 teaspoons salt
1/4 teaspoon black pepper
1/2 teaspoon paprika
Peanut oil

Wash and thoroughly dry the chicken. Beat the eggs in a small bowl and add 2 to 3 drops hot sauce. Place flour, salt, pepper and paprika in a re-sealable plastic bag. Dip chicken pieces into egg mixture and drop into the plastic bag with the flour mixture. Shake until chicken pieces are well coated.

Pour peanut oil 1/2 inch deep in a heavy skillet and heat until temperature reaches 375 degrees, or when a pinch of flour dropped onto the hot grease bubbles. Carefully place chicken into the skillet (temperature will drop to about 350 degrees), and fry 7 to 10 minutes. Turn each piece and fry an additional 7 to 10 minutes. Lower the heat, cover the skillet tightly and cook another 20 minutes. If the skillet cannot be covered tightly, add 1 to 2 tablespoons of water. Uncover for the last 5 to 10 minutes of cooking time to crisp the chicken. Drain chicken on paper towels.

Serves 6 to 8

cross country race cheese biscuits

1 stick butter
1/2 cup grated sharp Cheddar cheese
1 cup sifted all-purpose flour
1/8 teaspoon garlic salt
1/8 teaspoon red pepper
1 cup unsweetened puffed rice cereal

In a large bowl, cream the butter, add the cheese and mix thoroughly. In another bowl, sift the flour, garlic salt and red pepper together. Add the puffed rice cereal to the flour, coat well. Combine the flour mixture with the butter and cheese. Scoop mixture out onto a floured surface and knead until smooth. Roll into small balls and flatten with the palm of your hand. Place on baking sheet and bake at 370 degrees for about 20 minutes.

Serves 8 to 10

tack box celery and carrot sticks

15-ounce jar smooth peanut butter
5 tablespoons honey
1/4 cup chopped walnuts
1/4 cup raisins
1 bunch celery stalks
1 pound bag baby carrots

Mix peanut butter, honey, walnuts and raisins together in medium-size plastic bowl with a lid. Wash the celery and cut into 3 to 4-inch lengths. Spread a tablespoon of the peanut butter mixture into the center of each celery stick. Wrap each celery stick in a waxed paper strip and cover with a clinging plastic strip.

Serves 10 to 12

Sterling suggestion:
Instead of filling celery sticks, serve the peanut butter mixture with baby carrots.

spectator brownies

Two 1-ounce squares unsweetened chocolate
1/2 cup margarine
2 eggs
1 cup granulated sugar
1 teaspoon vanilla extract
1/2 cup all-purpose flour
1/2 tablespoon baking powder
1/2 cup chocolate chips
1/2 cup walnuts or pecans

Melt chocolate and margarine in a saucepan. In a mixing bowl, beat eggs and combine with the chocolate mixture. Add sugar and vanilla extract, blend. Add flour, baking powder, chocolate chips and walnuts. Mix well. Pour into a well-greased 8 by 8-inch pan. Bake in a preheated 325-degree oven for 35 minutes.

Serves 12

lunge line treat

2 cups pretzels
8 cups tender white popcorn
2 cups lightly salted whole or halved pecans

Place all ingredients in a large paper bag or bowl. Scoop 2-cup portions into individual sandwich bags.

Serves 6

The High Hope Steeplechase at the Kentucky Horse Park

In the spring, challengers at the High Hope Steeplechase race over brush and wooden jumps strategically placed along the landscape of the Kentucky Horse Park. The incredible gathering of horses and their riders brings many spectators to picnic or tailgate alongside the race course.

Prior to the day's race venue, The High Hope Steeplechase also hosts fun-filled children's activities, an arts and crafts fair, and the annual terrier dog trials. Jack Russell and other terrier breeds compete to see who is the fastest in their "field" as they attempt to catch a mechanically speeding wad of fake fur which they consider fair prey and a challenge to capture. It is truly a day well spent in the company of dogs and horses.

High Hope Steeplechase Brush Jump Picnic Basket Menu

Logan's Porch Lemonade
Sweet Kentucky Iced Tea
Olive Cheese Balls
Asparagus Rolls
Terrier Races Sandwich
Tomato and Basil Sandwiches
Steeplechase Pasta Salad
Clay's Cowboy Cookies

logan's porch lemonade

1/2 cup boiling water
1 1/2 cups granulated sugar
4 1/2 cups cold water
1 1/2 cups freshly squeezed lemon juice, about 12 lemons

Carefully pour the boiling water over the sugar in a bowl. Stir until the sugar dissolves. Mix in the cold water and lemon juice, stir and chill.

Serves 8

Sterling suggestion:
Nothing is more refreshing to tired travelers and weary riders.

sweet kentucky iced tea

2 large tea bags, decaffeinated or regular
16 cups boiling water, divided
2 cups sugar
Lemon slices or a mint sprig for garnish

Place tea bags in a large heat-proof container. Carefully pour 8 cups of boiling water over tea bags and steep for 5 minutes. In another container, place sugar and pour in the boiling water and stir until the remaining sugar is completely dissolved. Add this warm syrup to the steeped tea. Cool. Pour into tall tea glasses with lots of ice. Add lemon or mint sprig.

Serves 10

Sterling suggestion:
Southerners love sweet, rich-tasting tea.
It's the fullness of the syrup
rather than just mixing tea with sugar that
gives this regional drink its beloved
name "sweet tea."

cheese olive balls

15-ounce jar bacon cheese spread
4 tablespoons margarine
1/8 teaspoon hot sauce
1 teaspoon Worcestershire sauce
3/4 cup all-purpose flour
One 3-ounce jar pitted green olives, drained

In a mixing bowl, blend cheese spread and margarine until light and fluffy. Add hot sauce and Worcestershire sauce, and stir in flour. Mix well.

Use about 1 to 1 1/2 teaspoons of dough to shape around each olive. Place olive balls on an ungreased baking sheet. Bake 12 to 15 minutes at 400 degrees until light brown. Serve hot or at room temperature.

Serves 10 to 12

asparagus rolls

2 pounds asparagus, trimmed
1 loaf soft white bread, crusts removed
1 egg, beaten
4 ounces soft bleu cheese
8 ounces soft cream cheese, softened
2 sticks butter, melted

Cook asparagus in boiling water until crisp-tender. Drain and set aside. With a rolling pin, roll bread slices very thin. In a bowl, combine beaten egg with bleu cheese and cream cheese. Spread mixture on each slice of bread. Roll one asparagus stalk in bread slice. Dip into melted butter. Place seam side down on baking sheet and freeze one hour. When ready to bake, defrost slightly. Cut each roll into 3 pieces and bake in 400-degree oven for 15 minutes or until golden brown.

Serves 10 to 12

terrier races sandwich

dressing:

1/4 cup red wine vinegar
1 teaspoon dried oregano
1/2 teaspoon dry mustard
Dash of salt and pepper
1/2 cup extra virgin oil

sandwich:

1 loaf Italian bread with sesame seeds (24 inches in length),
   cut horizontally
1/4 cup each pepperoncini and cherry peppers, seeded
   and chopped
2 cups finely chopped lettuce
4 thinly sliced tomatoes
5 ounces thinly sliced cappicola
5 ounces thinly sliced salami
5 ounces thinly sliced country ham
5 ounces thinly sliced mortadella
5 ounces thinly sliced provolone cheese

In a small bowl, combine vinegar, oregano, mustard, salt and pepper. Stir to mix well. Whisk in the olive oil until well blended. On a work surface, lay out 3 long pieces of plastic wrap, placing them side by side and slightly overlapping. Place the bottom half of the loaf on the wrap. Spread the pepperoncini and cherry peppers over the bread. Evenly scatter the lettuce on the sandwich followed by the tomatoes. Drizzle with a few tablespoons of the dressing. Layer the meats over the tomatoes, distributing them equally. Top with a layer of cheese. Drizzle the remaining dressing over the cut side of the top of the loaf. Place on the sandwich and enclose in the plastic. Refrigerate for at least one hour or up to four hours for the flavors to develop. To serve, unwrap the sandwich and slice into large pieces; about 3 to 4 inches wide.

Serves 6 to 8

tomato and basil sandwiches

Ten baguettes
Extra-virgin olive oil
10 slices mozzarella cheese
4 large red ripe tomatoes
Salt and Pepper
1 clump fresh basil, leaves finely minced

Slice each baguette in half and drizzle each side with olive oil.
Place one slice mozzarella cheese on the bottom baguette half.
Cover the cheese with tomato slices, enough to adequately cover
the cheese, and generously add salt and pepper. Top with fresh
basil. Place the remaining bread on top and secure with an
extra-long toothpick.

Serves 10

steeplechase pasta salad

1 teaspoon salt
1 pound fusilli or penne pasta
1 tablespoon plus 1/3 cup extra virgin olive oil
1/4 cup finely chopped Italian parsley
3 tablespoons red wine vinegar
1/2 cup grated Parmesan cheese
5 cloves minced garlic
1/2 cup coarsely chopped basil
Salt and pepper
1 pound fresh mozzarella cheese, cut into 1-inch cubes
2 pounds ripe tomatoes, peeled, seeded and coarsely chopped

Bring a large pot two-thirds full of water to a boil over high heat and add salt. Add the pasta, stir well and cook until al dente (tender, but firm to the bite), about 7 to 10 minutes. Drain, place in a serving bowl and mix in 1 tablespoon olive oil.

In a mixing bowl, combine remaining ingredients. Pour over pasta and stir well to coat. Cover and chill until ready to serve.

Serves 4 to 6

clay's cowboy cookies

1/2 cup shortening
1/2 cup white sugar
1/2 cup brown sugar
1 large egg
1 cup all-purpose flour
1/4 teaspoon salt
1/4 teaspoon baking powder
1 cup rolled oats
1/2 teaspoon vanilla extract
1/2 package chocolate chips

Cream the shortening and sugars together in a large mixing bowl. Add egg and mix well. In another bowl, sift together flour, salt and baking powder. Add the oats and stir into the sugar mixture. Stir in vanilla and fold in the chocolate chips. Drop by teaspoonfuls onto a lightly greased baking sheet. Bake at 350 degrees for 15 minutes.

Serves 12 cookie eaters

Barn II:

Summer

The Red Mile Harness Track

1200 Red Mile Road Lexington, Kentucky 40505
(859) 255-0752 www.theredmile.com

The Red Mile, named for its one-mile red clay soil track, was established in 1875 and is the second oldest harness track in the world. The races for Standardbred horses are held in the summer and early fall. Powerful horses such as the tremendous trotter champion Greyhound and the crowd pleaser pacer Dan Patch, proved their unequalled prowess on the ground of The Red Mile. This track is home for the Kentucky Futurity Race which is comparable to its sister in Thoroughbred horse racing, The Kentucky Derby.

Saddlebred horses are showcased at the Red Mile in July. The Junior League of Lexington is an organization of trained volunteers whose purpose is to promote and support educational, historical and charitable programs throughout the area. For more than seven decades the Junior League has sponsored the celebrated Lexington Junior League Charity Horse Show. This distinguished equestrian venue is the first leg of the American Saddlebred Triple Crown attracting national and international horsemen. The Lexington Junior League Charity Horse Show is the largest outdoor Saddlebred event in the United States.

Lexington Junior League Blue Ribbon Box Lunch

Pecan and Gorgonzola-Coated Grapes
Champion Chicken Spinach Strawberry Salad
Trophy Fudge

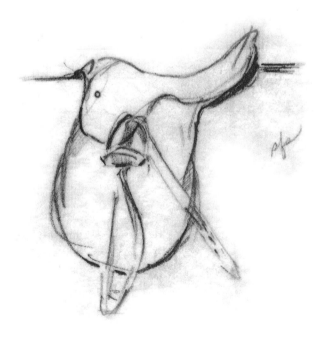

pecan and gorgonzola-coated grapes

1 cup finely chopped pecans
6 ounces crumbled gorgonzola cheese
4 ounces cream cheese
22 seedless red grapes

Spread the pecans on a baking sheet and toast in a 325-degree oven for 5 minutes. In a bowl, cream the gorgonzola and cream cheese with a wooden spoon or electric mixer.

Wrap each grape in one tablespoon of cheese mixture, shaping with hands. Roll the covered grapes in pecans and place on a serving tray. Chill for 30 minutes until coating is firm.

Serves 5

champion chicken spinach strawberry salad

3/4 cup sugar
1 teaspoon salt
1 teaspoon dry mustard
1/3 cup red wine vinegar
1 teaspoon onion juice
1 cup vegetable oil
1 tablespoon poppy seeds
1 cup sliced almonds
6 cups torn fresh spinach
1 quart strawberries, sliced
3 kiwifruit, peeled and sliced
3 cups chopped, cooked chicken

Process the sugar, salt, mustard, vinegar, and onion juice in a blender until smooth. Turn blender on high and add vegetable oil in a slow stream. Pour mixture into a serving bowl and stir in poppy seeds. Chill.

Spread almonds on a baking sheet and bake in a 350-degree oven for 3 to 5 minutes. Place spinach on plates and top with strawberries, kiwi and chicken, and toasted almonds. Gently drizzle the dressing on top and toss to coat.

Serves 6 to 8

Sterling suggestion:
An attractive way to serve this at a picnic is to use a florist's clear orchid corsage box. Line the container with fresh spinach leaves and spoon individual servings of the Champion Chicken Spinach Strawberry Salad on top of the leaves. Drizzle with the dressing. Place the grapes in a small cupcake paper and tuck into one corner of the corsage box while slipping a fresh bakery croissant into another corner.

Wrap the entire box and cutlery with a wide satin ribbon.

trophy fudge

3 to 6 ounces chocolate chips
14-ounce can sweetened condensed milk
1 1/2 teaspoons vanilla extract
1/2 cup chopped nuts, optional
Dash of salt

In a saucepan, melt chocolate chips with sweetened condensed milk. Remove from heat and add remaining ingredients. Pour into a square baking dish that has been lined with waxed paper. Cool until hardened and cut into squares.

Serves 10 to 12

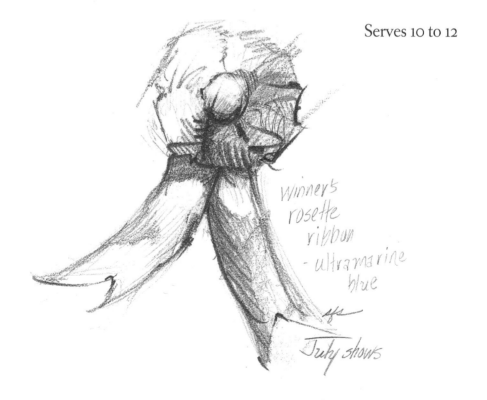

winner's
rosette
ribbon
- ultramarine
blue

July shows

Summer Horse Sales Cocktail Party

Handicapper's Hors d'oeuvres
Furlong Mushrooms in Filo Shells
Sterling Stirrups Shrimp Mold
Buyers Blue Cheese & Bacon Puffs
My Mare's Mini Hot Brown Appetizer
Hot Walkers Baked Apricots
Walnut Bourbon Balls
Kentucky Bourbon Slushy
Kentucky Bourbon on the Rocks
Kentucky Chardonnay Wine

handicapper's hors d'oeuvres

1 pound bacon
8 ounces pitted dates
8 ounces slivered almonds

Cook bacon in a microwave for 10 minutes or until partially cooked. Remove, drain and cut bacon strips into thirds. Stuff each date with an almond and wrap in 1/3 piece of bacon and secure with a toothpick.

Serves 12 to 15

furlong mushrooms in filo shells

3 tablespoons finely chopped shallots
6 ounces Portobello and button mushrooms, chopped
2 tablespoons all-purpose flour
3/4 to 1 cup heavy cream
4 tablespoons grated Parmesan cheese
1 package frozen filo shells, thawed

In a skillet, sauté the shallots and mushrooms for 3 to 5 minutes. Blend in the flour, cream and cheese and cook until mixture is thickened. Spoon mixture into filo shells and bake at 350 degrees for 15 minutes.

Serves 8

silver stirrup shrimp mold

2 pounds cooked shrimp, deveined
Four 8-ounce packages cream cheese, softened
1 small onion, finely chopped
1/4 cup finely chopped celery
1 teaspoon Worcestershire sauce
1 teaspoon garlic powder
Dash of steak sauce
Dash of fresh lemon juice
Paprika
Lettuce or other salad greens for garnish

Wash and drain the shrimp and chop into small pieces. In a large mixing bowl, combine remaining ingredients, except paprika and lettuce. Fold in the shrimp. Line a food mold with plastic wrap. Spoon the mixture into the mold, pressing down gently to form the shape of the mold. Cover and place into the refrigerator for at least 1 hour. To serve, invert the mold onto a serving platter lined with the large lettuce leaves. Sprinkle with paprika.

Serves 10 to 12

buyer's blue cheese & bacon puffs

1 1/2 cups water
3/4 cup butter or margarine
1 1/2 cups all-purpose flour
1/2 teaspoon salt
1/2 teaspoon ground black pepper
1/4 teaspoon ground red pepper
6 large eggs
8 ounces blue cheese, crumbed
8 to 10 bacon strips, cooked and crumbled
4 green onions, finely chopped

Bring water and butter to a boil in a heavy saucepan over medium heat. Add flour, salt, black pepper and red pepper. Cook; beating with a wooden spoon, until mixture leaves sides of pan and forms a smooth ball of dough. Remove from heat and cool 5 minutes. Add eggs, one at a time, beating well with spoon after each addition. Beat in cheese, bacon and chopped green onions. Drop dough by rounded teaspoonfuls 2 inches apart onto lightly greased baking sheets. Bake at 400 degrees for 20 to 25 minutes or until golden. Puffs will be moist in center. Serve warm or at room temperature.

Serves 36

my mare's mini hot brown appetizer

2 chicken bouillon cubes
1/2 cup hot water
1 1/2 cups half-and-half
6 tablespoons unsalted butter
4 tablespoons all-purpose flour
2 cups Swiss cheese, shredded
8 bacon strips, cooked, crumbled
1 French baguette, 1/4 to 1/2-inch slices
1 pound country ham, sliced
1 pound turkey, sliced
1/4 small onion, sliced thin
Parsley for garnish

In a large measuring cup, dissolve the bouillon cubes in hot water. Cool slightly before slowly adding the half-and-half. Melt butter in a saucepan and add flour, whisking until the mixture is creamy. Add the bouillon mixture while continuing to whisk until the sauce bubbles and thickens. Add the Swiss cheese and stir until smooth. If sauce is too thick, simply add water and heat to thin. Spray baking dish with cooking spray and place bread slices on bottom. Layer ham, turkey and onion on the bread. Cover with cheese sauce and top with the crumbled bacon. Bake at 350 degrees for 10 to 15 minutes until lightly browned and bubbly. Garnish with parsley.

Serves 8 to 10

hot walker's baked apricots

8 cups canned apricot halves, drained
1 1/2 cups packed brown sugar
1/2 cup Kentucky bourbon
1 1/2 sticks butter, melted
2 1/2 cups crushed butter crackers

Spray a large baking dish with non-stick cooking spray. Spread well-drained apricots in the dish. Sprinkle with brown sugar, then drizzle with bourbon. Combine melted butter with cracker crumbs and sprinkle over apricots. Bake at 325 degrees for 25 to 30 minutes.

Serves 8

top line is important

walnut bourbon balls

1 cup powdered sugar
2 1/2 cups finely crushed vanilla wafers
2 tablespoons cocoa
1 cup finely chopped walnuts
3 tablespoons white corn syrup
1/4 cup Kentucky bourbon
Extra powdered sugar for coating

Combine powdered sugar, vanilla wafers, cocoa and walnuts in a large mixing bowl. Add syrup and bourbon. Work into one-inch balls and roll in powdered sugar.

Makes 3 1/2 dozen

kentucky bourbon slushy

12-ounce can frozen lemonade
12-ounce can frozen orange juice
Three 12-ounce cans filled with cold water
1 cup sugar
5 tablespoons instant tea
2 cups Kentucky bourbon
Lemon-lime soft drink

Combine all ingredients except the lemon-lime soft drink in a large plastic container with lid. Place in freezer, stirring every 2 to 6 hours. To serve, put several tablespoons of "slush" in a glass and pour in just enough lemon-lime soft drink to fill glass.

kentucky bourbon on the rocks

Like many states, Kentucky makes a distilled spirit known as whiskey. However, Kentucky has Bourbon County in its Bluegrass Region from which a drink made predominately from corn and aged only in oak barrels for a specific number of years, sprang into existence in the 19th century and was given its county's name. "Fine Bourbon" whiskey, or "Bourbon" is another original of this diverse state.

Kentucky bourbon
Ice cubes to 1/2 fill the glass

Fill a four-ounce clear glass tumbler half full of ice. Pour 2 jiggers of bourbon over ice. This is called "real sipping bourbon whiskey."

kentucky chardonnay wine

Much of Bluegrass farmland is dark, fertile soil. When handled knowingly with an understanding of tricky weather patterns and growing season timetables, the ground can be very productive. Many landowners have turned from raising tobacco to growing crops such as soy beans and heirloom garden vegetables. Hardworking farmers and enterprising gardeners have begun to research and develop outstanding vineyards as well.

The grapes of these vineyards yield an array of enticing wines being marketed in stores, select food and wine shops, restaurants and taverns.

Barn III:
Autumn

Sterling bit: If you see a horse with a red ribbon woven into its tail, stand clear since this animal may have the propensity to kick.

Foxhunting

Foxhunters adore foxhounds and have an affinity for the breed, always referring to the animals as hounds. You may say, "I love your hound," but avoid, "I like your dog."

People who "ride to the hunt" have three loves: Kentucky's farmland, horses and hounds. Foxhunting is a sport which stretches between September and March. It involves a skilled rider on a well-schooled horse capable of jumping ditches, streams, fences and fallen trees or bramble. They gallop for miles to the sight and sound of hounds who are giving chase to a fox or coyote. The baying of the hounds alerts the huntsmen that there is quarry in the countryside, and beckons the foxhunters to follow for a glimpse of a coy fox or the larger, courser coyote.

There is a specific dress attire and formal protocol associated with foxhunting. The Master of the Hounds wears a highly visible red or scarlet hunt coat. This position is not given or taken lightly because the individual is experienced and recognized as a leader should others need assistance or advice on the field or if a landowner has a question. Tall leather riding boots protect the legs from rough foliage or thorns in deep thickets. Riding helmets, covered in velvet and detailed with a ribbon, are a safety requirement. As a social club, members abide by the organization's rules and traditions, of which many were established more than 100 years ago.

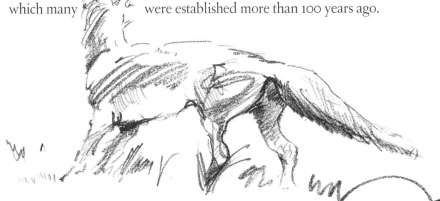

careful

Hunt Club Scarlet Coat Breakfast

Hill Topper's Bloody Mary Cocktails
Foxhound Frosty Fruit
Country Ham Balls
Huntsman Breakfast Cups
Poppy Seed Muffins
Gallop on Gingerbread with Lemon Sauce

hill topper's bloody mary cocktails

1 1/2 teaspoons horseradish
2 ounces vodka
1 tablespoon lemon juice
1/2 teaspoon Worcestershire sauce
3 drops hot sauce
4 ounces tomato juice

Squeeze dry the horseradish. Combine all of the ingredients in a shaker and serve over ice. Garnish with cracked pepper, celery stalk and green olive.

Serves 4

Sterling suggestion:
Dress a wooden toothpick with a large green olive and lime slice to garnish the cocktail, or, cut celery into six-inch lengths to use as swizzle sticks.

foxhound frosty fruit

2 cups water
20-ounce can pineapple tidbits, plus juice
2 cups sugar
6 bananas, chopped
12 ounces frozen orange juice concentrate
10-ounce jar cherries, chopped
11-ounce can mandarin oranges, chopped

Combine all ingredients in a large pitcher and mix well. Pour into 12 plastic cups and freeze. Remove from freezer 30 minutes before serving.

Serves 12

country ham balls

2 pounds ground country ham
1 cup dry bread crumbs
1 pound pork sausage
2 eggs, beaten
Milk
2 cups brown sugar
1 cup water
1 1/2 tablespoons prepared mustard
1 cup white wine vinegar

Combine country ham, bread crumbs and sausage in a large mixing bowl. Add eggs, and enough milk to make mixture easy to roll into small balls. Place balls in a greased dish.

Combine brown sugar, water, mustard, and vinegar in a saucepan and bring to a boil. Pour over country ham balls and bake at 350 degrees until firm.

Serves 10 to 12

huntsman breakfast cups

Two 3-ounce packages cream cheese, softened
2 tablespoons milk
1 large egg
1/2 cup shredded Swiss cheese
1 green onion, chopped
12-ounce can biscuits
6 bacon slices, cooked and crumbled

In a large bowl, beat cream cheese, milk and egg at medium speed with an electric mixer until blended. Stir in Swiss cheese and green onion, set aside. Separate biscuits into 1 piece portions and pat each one into a 5-inch circle. Press on the bottom and up sides of greased muffin cups, forming a 1/4- inch edge. Sprinkle evenly with half of the bacon and spoon cream cheese mixture evenly on top. Bake at 375 degrees for 20 minutes or until set. Sprinkle with remaining bacon and garnish with sliced green onion.

Serves 10

poppy seed muffins

1 1/2 cups baking mix
1 tablespoon poppy seeds
1/2 cup sugar
1 egg, beaten
3/4 cup sour cream
1 teaspoon vanilla extract

Combine all ingredients in a large mixing bowl and mix until moist.
Fill greased muffin tins about half full. Bake at 400 degrees for
20 minutes.

Serves 12

gallop-on gingerbread with lemon sauce

1 cup shortening
1 cup sugar
1 cup molasses
2 eggs
3 cups all-purpose flour
1 1/2 teaspoons baking soda
1 1/2 teaspoons salt
1 teaspoon ground ginger
1 teaspoon ground cinnamon
1 cup hot water

In large mixing bowl, beat the shortening, sugar, molasses and eggs until well blended. In a separate bowl, combine flour, baking soda, salt, ginger and cinnamon; add to molasses mixture alternately with hot water. Pour into greased 9 by 13-inch baking pan. Bake at 350 degrees for 35 to 40 minutes or until toothpick inserted near the center comes out clean. Cool on wire rack.

Serves 10

lemon sauce

1/2 cup granulated sugar
1 tablespoon cornstarch
1 cup boiling water
2 tablespoons butter
1 1/2 teaspoons lemon juice
Dash of salt
1 teaspoon lemon zest

Combine sugar and cornstarch in a saucepan. Gradually add boiling water and boil 5 minutes. Remove from heat and add other ingredients. Serve the sauce hot.

Sterling Suggestion:
To create a leaf plate charger for an autumn meal, purchase a cardboard circle (one for separating cake layers sold at chain stores in the craft section). Using a hot glue gun, adhere magnolia or fall leaves around the complete circle edge. Overlap so that no white space remains. Add berries, if desired. Place a dinner plate in the center.

Kentucky Trail Riding

The foothills of the ruggedly beautiful Appalachian Mountains pierce the eastern part of Kentucky, and gorgeous deep woods encompass other areas of the state as well. Riding trails found meandering through these woods and hills are a good choice for horse lovers seeking a day, an overnight or weekend, in the company of a gifted pleasure horse. Some people find paradise in guided trail rides; others like to saddle their own horse to ride over miles of marked trails.

The key to the success of the Kentucky trail ride is having a smooth-gaited walking or pleasure horse. The Mountain or Rocky Mountain horses are ideal choices for trail riding. Both breeds are related by genes from horses bred for generations within rural Kentucky. The horses differ in coat and mane color. The Registered Rocky Mountain horse has a chocolate colored coat and a flaxen mane. Standards have been set for conformation, color and disposition by their perspective associations yet they share several marked traits. These animals are naturally gaited, quiet in disposition, surefooted, noted for their endurance, and acclimated to the state's unpredictable and sometimes raw weather patterns.

Characteristically gentle pleasure horses are comfortable to ride because of an extremely smooth gait known as a running walk. This gliding four-count movement covers rough ground deftly and quickly. Riders of pleasure horses or gaited walking horse breeds travel more than seven miles in one hour and can sustain a three- to six-hour ride depending upon the weather and terrain. Lunch is usually a pleasant stop along the trail and the evening campfire meal is welcoming. Happy trails!

Autumn Trail Ride Saddlebag Grub

Camp Cook's Crock Pot Beans
Corn Pones
Palomino Potato Soup
Bed Down Beer Biscuits
Walking Horse Cake

camp cook's slow-cooked beans

Two 13- to 15.5-ounce cans baked beans
1 cup chopped celery
1 pound ground chuck, browned and drained
1 medium onion, chopped and browned
1 green pepper, chopped
1 tablespoon mustard
1 tablespoon Worcestershire sauce
1/4 to 1/2 cup each ketchup, barbecue sauce and brown sugar
1/2 cup water

Combine all ingredients in a slow cooker. Stir and cook on low about 4 hours.

Serves 8

corn pones

1 1/2 cups water
1/2 teaspoon salt
1 to 2 tablespoons bacon fat
1 1/2 cups white cornmeal
1/4 cup shortening

In a saucepan, bring water to almost boiling. Add salt and bacon fat and let come to a full boil. Remove from heat and slowly pour cornmeal into water. Stir into a batter. Spoon shortening into a heavy iron skillet and heat until very hot. Carefully drop batter from a long handled spoon into hot skillet and flatten cakes. When brown on one side, turn. Add more shortening if needed and brown on other side.

Serves 4 to 6

Sterling suggestion:
Season your cast iron by rubbing it with a light coat of oil and bake for 30 minudtes to 1 hour at 400 degrees.

palomino potato soup

8 slices bacon
1 cup chopped onions
2 cups diced potatoes
2 stalks celery, coarsely chopped
3 carrots, chopped
1 teaspoon salt
1/8 teaspoon pepper
10 3/4-ounce can cream of chicken soup
1 cup sour cream
1 1/2 cups milk
1 1/2 cups water

Cut 8 slices of bacon into small pieces and cook in a skillet until almost done. Add onion and sauté with bacon. In a large pot, cook potatoes, celery, carrots, salt and pepper, until vegetables are soft. Add bacon mixture. Mix in soup, sour cream and milk. Stir and let simmer. You may need to add water as soup thickens or if you reheat it the next day.

Serves 8 to 10

bed down beer biscuits

3/4 cup beer, room temperature
1 1/2 cups biscuit mix
1/4 teaspoon salt
1 teaspoon sugar

In a mixing bowl, combine all ingredients and mix well. Spoon ingredients into greased muffin tin. Bake at 425 degrees for 15 minutes.

Serves 6 to 8

walking horse cake

2 cups all-purpose flour
2 cups sugar
2 teaspoons baking soda
1 1/2 cups pecans
20-ounce can crushed pineapple
1 teaspoon vanilla extract
1 cup maraschino cherries

Lightly grease and flour an 8- by 8-inch rectangular cake pan.
Combine all ingredients in a large mixing bowl and mix well.
Pour into prepared cake pan. Bake at 350 degrees for 45 minutes.

Serves 8 to 10

walking horse cake icing

8 ounces cream cheese, softened
1 stick butter, softened
2 cups powdered sugar
2 teaspoons vanilla extract

Combine all ingredients in a medium mixing bowl and mix well
with an electric mixer. Spread over cooled cake.

Barn IV:
Winter

sfs
broodmare in foal

Foaling Season

Foaling season is an important time for horse owners and breeders. Thoroughbred horses typically foal between January and May thus the term "foaling season." Thoroughbred foals born during the year officially become one year old on January first following its birth. January first is its birthday. A Thoroughbred foal less than two years old is a yearling. Many breeds of broodmares are monitored as the birth time approaches to ensure that all goes well. Foals are often born in the wee hours of the morning, and it is not uncommon for the people on duty to lose sleep as nature, taking its course, does not look at a clock.

For this reason, the following recipes are simple to prepare and convenient to carry to the foaling barn whether on a paper plate or in an insulated travel mug. A weary, hungry watch person will be grateful to have something satisfying to sip and munch while waiting for a mother to go into labor.

Foaling Barn Watch Comfort Foods

Barn Stall Biscuits
Midnight Tomato Soup
Colt Popcorn Balls
Fillies Fried Apple Pies
Long Night Hot Chocolate
Happy Hooves Birthday Celebration Cake

barn stall biscuits

1 stick butter or margarine, melted
2 tablespoons poppy seeds
2 tablespoons chopped onion
1 1/2 tablespoons dry mustard
1 teaspoon Worcestershire sauce
Two 12-ounce packages ready-made biscuits
  or rolls in aluminum pans
1/2 pound ready-to-serve minced ham
16 ounces grated Swiss cheese

Melt butter in a saucepan and stir in poppy seeds, onion, dry mustard, and Worcestershire sauce. Slice biscuits or rolls in half and brush with butter mixture. Layer the ham and cheese and return to pan. Pour the remaining butter mixture over the top. Bake at 350 degrees for 15 minutes.

Serves 8 to 10

midnight tomato soup

2 tablespoons butter
1 small onion, finely chopped
Three 16-ounce cans whole tomatoes
1 quart chicken stock
1/4 cup sugar
1 pint half-and-half
3 tablespoons dill weed or a sprig of fresh dill

Melt butter in a large stock pot and sauté onions until soft. Roughly chop tomatoes, reserving the juice. Add tomatoes, juice, stock and sugar to the pot. Bring to a boil and then lower heat to simmer. Slowly whisk the half-and-half into the soup and continue simmering for 20 minutes. Garnish with dill weed or a sprig of fresh dill.

Serves 10

colt popcorn balls

1 cup sugar
1 teaspoon salt
1/3 cup water
1/4 cup butter
1/3 cup light corn syrup
1 teaspoon vanilla extract
7 cups popped corn

Combine sugar, salt, water, butter and syrup in a saucepan and simmer over medium heat. Cook to 250 degrees or until a few drops placed in cold water form a hard ball. Remove from heat and stir in vanilla.

Pour in a thin stream over the popped corn stirring constantly to mix well. Lightly butter your hands and shape the mixture into balls.

Serves 12

fillies fried apple pies

12-ounce can biscuits
21-ounce can apple pie filling
1/4 cup salad oil
2 tablespoons butter
Sugar

With a rolling pin, flatten each biscuit into a circle. Place about 2 tablespoons of apple pie filling on one half of the circle. Fold the other half of the flattened biscuit over the filling. Dip a fork in flour and press the edges together to keep the filling inside. Continue until all the pastry and fruit is used.

In a heavy skillet, heat oil and butter to 375 degrees, fry pies, two or three at a time until golden brown. Drain and dust with sugar.

Serves 10

long night hot chocolate

1 cup milk
1-ounce square semisweet chocolate
1/4 teaspoon vanilla extract
1 teaspoon sugar
2 tablespoons sweetened whipped cream

In a small saucepan over low heat, warm milk until bubbles appear around the edges. Remove from heat. Chop chocolate and beat into milk with a wire whisk or hand beater. When chocolate is melted, add vanilla and sugar and stir to combine. Pour into a cup or mug and top with whipped cream.

Serves 1

happy hooves
birthday celebration cake

Each newborn foal having stood and nursed from its dam for the first time is extraordinary. It is a reason to celebrate. Once all is quiet in the barn and the sleep-deprived horsemen have gotten some well-deserved rest, a special birthday cake is in order to honor the proud new equine momma.

4 cups horse oats
1 cup molasses
13.3-ounce jar smooth peanut butter
Peppermint sticks or whole carrots

Mix all ingredients in a large bowl. Press the mixture into a round cake shape and place on a disposable or aluminum platter.

Sterling suggestion: To decorate the horse cake, place a small amount of molasses on the peppermint sticks and press vertically all around the cake. Wrap a wide burlap ribbon or braided twine around the middle of the peppermint sticks to secure and tie in a bow. Whole carrots may be substituted for peppermint sticks.